Maintaining motivation:
strategies for improving retention rates
in adult language classes

Other titles in the NETWORD series

NETWORD 1 — A toolkit for talking: strategies for independent reading
by Duncan Sidwell
Discusses classroom conditions and teaching techniques which will encourage students to progress to independent use of the foreign language. Principles of methodology are supported by many examples of information gap and graded activities.
240 x 210mm, paperback, 72 pages, ISBN 1 874016 17 8, £7.50

NETWORD 2 — Language games and activities
by John Langran and Sue Purcell
Each of thirteen games in the book is described in detail, with full instructions for exploitation, and is given as an example of a principle or strategy which can be re-used with a different language, at different levels, with different groups and for different purposes.
240 x 210mm, paperback, 64 pages, ISBN 1 874016 23 2, £7.50

NETWORD 3 — Mixed-ability teaching: meeting learners' needs
by Susan Ainslie
Offers strategies for differentiation between individual learners in a group, which will help the learner to achieve his or her learning potential. A range of suggested practical activities will be useful for individual tutors or as a basis for group work.
240 x 210mm, paperback, 60 pages, ISBN 1 874016 33 X, £7.50

NETWORD 4 — Assessing adult learners
by Susan Ainslie and Alwena Lamping
This book looks at ways of integrating assessment into the teaching programme. It offers practical suggestions on creating and choosing appropriate assessment materials, collecting evidence of competence, assessment techniques and managing assessment in the classroom. The final chapter considers formal accreditation and provides guidelines on how to choose from the range of accreditation on offer in the UK.
240 x 210mm, paperback, 68 pages, ISBN 1 874016 39 9, £7.50

CILT publications are available through all good booksellers and from the national network of Comenius Centres, Scottish CILT, and Northern Ireland CILT (further details on 0171 379 5101). Orders may also be sent to CILT's distributor: Grantham Book Services Ltd, Isaac Newton Way, Alma Park Industrial Estate, Grantham, Lincs NG31 9SD. Telephone credit card orders to: 01476 567 421, fax orders to 01476 592 939.

Visitors to the Information and Resources Library at CILT, 20 Bedfordbury, London, WC2N 4LB (telephone 0171 379 5110) receive a 10% discount on all CILT publications, CILT Direct subscribers receive a 15% discount.

NETWORD 5

TEACHING LANGUAGES TO ADULTS

Maintaining motivation:
strategies for improving retention rates
in adult language classes

Alwena Lamping and Christine Ball

Cartoons by Joanne Bond

CiLT

Centre for Information
on Language Teaching and Research

The views expressed in this publication are the authors' and do not necessarily represent those of CILT.

First published 1996
© 1996 Centre for Information on Language Teaching and Research
ISBN 1 874016 68 2

A catalogue record for this book is available from the British Library
Cover by Neil Alexander
Printed in Great Britain by Bourne Press Ltd

Published by the Centre for Information on Language Teaching and Research,
20 Bedfordbury, Covent Garden, London WC2N 4LB

Contents

Introduction

The pleasures of teaching languages to adults stem largely from the fact that adults are volunteers – they choose to give up their free time to learn a language, they want to learn and they appreciate the need for learning.

But, as volunteers, they are not compelled to attend classes, and many stop doing so before the end of their course. It was commonplace in the past for numbers in adult language classes to dwindle very rapidly after the first flush of enthusiasm had worn off, and many classes starting in September barely survived until Christmas. This was seen as disappointing but inevitable and perfectly acceptable.

Times have changed. Adult learners are still volunteers, but now that the funding of classes is wholly dependent on high retention and achievement rates we can no longer claim that drop-out is of no great consequence.

A survey into the reasons for language learners dropping out of classes was undertaken in Mid-Cheshire College in 1993 and disseminated in the Autumn 1994 edition of *NETWORD*. It provoked a wide-ranging response and was the starting point for this book. Many tutors who had previously dismissed the problem as inevitable, or preferred not to admit it was happening to them, joined in the debate and it became obvious that this is an issue which concerns a great number of people today.

National concern

This book:

- explores the reasons why learners leave a course;
- considers how to sustain their initial motivation;
- proposes strategies to employ at various key times;
- provides examples of relevant documentation;
- offers practical ideas.

It is not about crisis management; it does not offer a miracle cure allowing a tutor to re-assemble in April all the learners who have drifted away between November and March. The aim of this book is to suggest as many measures as possible to prevent them dropping out in the first place.

Some factors are obviously beyond a tutor's influence. Not even the most riveting course is immune to learners who suffer illness or bereavement or who are relocated at work. There will always be some people who find that, for one reason or another, language learning is beyond them. But these are not the only reasons for learners dropping out, and there **are** things we can do to help retain our learners.

FEFC funding

Not only are high drop-out rates detrimental for tutors and students, they also have a direct effect on a college's financial stability.

Course fees paid by students cover only a small proportion of costs, and colleges rely on various sources of funding for the bulk of their income. The Further Education Funding Council (FEFC) is the major source of funding for many colleges which are then bound by the terms of that funding.

The FEFC provides a standard amount for each person who enrols on a vocational course. The actual amount depends on factors such as the type of course, the course length and the qualification. A college calculates its budget from the numbers enrolled and receives its funding from the FEFC in instalments. However, there are conditions attached and **payment of the instalments is dependent on students continuing to attend the course.** There is no distinction made between someone who drops out of a course on a whim and the unemployed person who leaves because he has found employment; no allowances made for those who leave because of a personal tragedy or those who move away from the area.

The system is far from ideal, but what it has done is to focus our attention on an important issue and oblige us to do more to ensure that learners complete their courses and achieve what they set out to achieve.

(For more specific detail of the FEFC funding mechanism at the time of writing, see the Appendix on p70.)

It is hoped that the book will be of interest to individual tutors of languages to adults, trainers of language tutors and also to those in charge of the adult language provision.

Why do retention rates matter?

The spotlight is currently on retention rates because of the link with funding, but there are clearly other compelling reasons for ensuring that learners complete their course.

We all know the feeling of satisfaction gained from teaching a group of enthusiastic, well-motivated adults and sharing in their progress and their sense of achievement. It is crucial to that satisfaction that the learners carry on attending classes regularly, but it is not just for our own self-esteem or professional pride that we need to encourage them to do so. The effects of dwindling numbers are detrimental for everyone concerned and once numbers start to drop, the class can embark on a depressing downward spiral:

Those who leave obviously lose out. Having paid their fees and enrolled with high hopes and ambitions, this one experience of language learning could well have put them off for life.

It has a **negative effect on the tutor.** Nothing can be more demoralising for a tutor than to realise that learners are no longer attending classes. The instinctive reaction is to blame oneself and self-confidence plummets.

When a tutor begins to doubt his/her ability, the **'buzz' or momentum goes from the lessons,** instantly making them less attractive and easier to miss.

As soon as the buzz goes, the **enthusiasm of remaining students starts to wane.**

They in turn can start drifting away . .

Why do they drop out?

Chapter 1

It is obvious that this is the key question we should be asking if we are to maintain high retention rates and persuade wavering students to stay the course. In the Mid-Cheshire study the question was put directly and anonymously to students who had stopped attending language classes. The replies were wide ranging, and this first chapter gives an overview of the picture which emerged from them and the conclusions which we can draw from the information obtained.

Student motivation is a major factor in successful language learning, and since an increased understanding of the subject will undoubtedly assist in addressing retention rates, we should first try to establish the reasons learners have for wishing to learn a language.

Why do they enrol?

The motivation that drives adults to enrol in September for their chosen language stems from many different sources. It could be argued that there are as many reasons for learning as there are learners. Opposite we see a few of the most common reasons offered in answer to the question *Why did you enrol?*

We tend to assume that people decide to enrol on a language course in order to get by on holiday or because they need to use a foreign language at work. Although these are indeed two of the motivating factors, they are by no means the only ones. Many people enrol because they like the idea of learning a language for its own sake. They may want to build on skills they already have or to acquire new skills. Some simply want to stretch themselves in a new direction, while others hope to make new friends with a common interest.

The students targeted in the survey had already abandoned their course. Do students who drop out perhaps have different motives for enrolling from other students? Is this why they don't complete the course?

It seemed a good way to make friends.

We have an apartment in Portugal.

It would look good on my CV.

I wanted to learn a language – Spanish seemed quite easy.

I have friends in France. I'd like to be able to speak to them more easily.

I did some German in school and wanted to take it further.

I needed more confidence.

It would be great to be able to speak to people on holiday.

Several surveys have been carried out among adult language learners, notably the 1991 Lancashire survey (Ainslie, 1991). This was consulted to check whether the students questioned (still attending classes) had substantially different reasons for enrolling from students who had dropped out. No differences emerged, so we can assume that, with few exceptions, the students' initial motivation has little bearing on why they drop out.

So why is it that, a few weeks after enrolling, for some students though not for all, the initial enthusiasm wanes and attendance becomes erratic or ceases altogether? After all, they all had similar reasons for enrolling. Why does it happen?

What goes wrong?

Opposite we see some of the reasons given by students for abandoning language courses. They fall easily into three categories:

- changes in home or work commitments;
- changes in personal motivation;
- unhappiness about some aspect of the class.

Changes in home or work commitments

The very factors which make adult language learners so interesting and enjoyable to teach — their varied experiences, interests and backgrounds — are the ones which make it difficult for them to commit themselves to regular attendance at an evening class.

They are part-time students, and generally their language class has to come second to work, family, social and other commitments. Some of these factors are completely outside our control as tutors. There is nothing we can do to keep a student who has to relocate to a different part of the country. There is little we can do when someone suddenly finds themselves the sole carer of an elderly relative who cannot be left alone.

Changes in personal motivation

This category, too, would appear to be beyond the tutor's scope. If a student has enrolled on a German class to prepare for a trip to Germany, and the trip is cancelled, then the initial motivation has gone. If a student joins a language course to enhance career prospects and is subsequently not successful in a job interview, where then is the motivation to continue with the course?

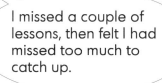

I missed a couple of lessons, then felt I had missed too much to catch up.

Pressure of work was just too great.

I didn't feel I had enough opportunity to speak.

I divorced and moved house. It caused havoc!

All the others were better than me.

It was too difficult for me – too much grammar.

The class was too big and we all seemed at different levels.

I couldn't get a babysitter – anyway I was finding it too hard.

We might conclude from this that there is nothing the tutor can do to influence the decision of a student who abandons the course as a result of a factor in these two categories, but when students are thoroughly enjoying the course and the experience is outstripping their expectations they will move heaven and earth to keep coming. Many tutors will know of students with problems at work who claim that it is only their language class on Tuesday evening which keeps them sane.

Unhappiness with some aspect of the class

Many of the replies in this category related to the level of the class:

- too wide a range of abilities within the class;
- too many stages of learning within the class;
- beginners' classes full of non-beginners;
- level too difficult — targeted at the more advanced learners.

Others were more difficult to classify:

- class too big — not enough tutor attention;
- everyone else progressing much faster;
- too difficult;
- not enough grammar;
- too much grammar.

It might appear from this that the tutor is in a position to dissuade only a tiny minority of early leavers from leaving. But is this the complete picture?

Do students tell us the whole story?

Accepting the above analysis at face value, only about a third of those learners who drop out do so because they are unhappy with some aspect of their class. Of that third, only a few give reasons closely connected with teaching and learning. Are low retention rates therefore inevitable in language classes? Or are we lulling ourselves into a false sense of complacency? Perhaps we should be more objective, and wary of accepting at face value some of the reasons offered to us for abandoning a course. Are we convinced that some of the reasons which appear to be in the first two categories do not in reality derive from the third category?

When disenchanted learners say . . .

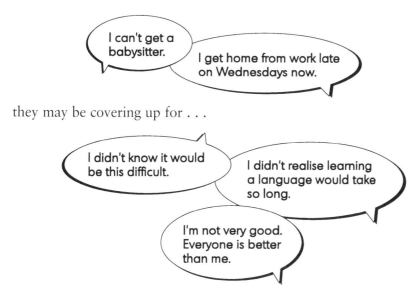

they may be covering up for . . .

In other words, their expectations of the language course had not been at all realistic.

Experienced teachers know that adult learners bring with them to the course much more than just enthusiasm and issues relating to their work and family. They come laden with preconceived ideas about teaching and learning.

- Many come with the notion that language learning is a passive occupation; that they need only sit and listen or sit and read, and magically they will soon be able to speak. The teacher takes all the responsibility, just as they remember from schooldays.
- Others have the idea that they will be able to speak fluently within weeks, which is hardly surprising given the way many 'language courses' are advertised in the media.

And it is when their experience fails to match up to their expectations that enthusiasm wanes.

This would go a long way towards explaining why beginners' classes generally suffer worse retention rates than classes at higher levels. It cannot be that babysitter problems, late shifts and the care of elderly relatives are unique to beginners.

What do the learners expect?

Learners at Levels 2 and above already know what it means to learn a language; they appreciate the commitment required, they know what happens in the language classroom, they are comfortable with the process. They are also less prone to abandoning their courses.

So . . . do we simply accept that beginners' classes will automatically have worse retention rates? Or do we try to ensure that their expectations are more realistic? Can we make the reality a positive, enjoyable experience which they will not wish to give up?

How do we achieve this?   In the chapters which follow, we offer suggestions on how this might be achieved. We propose strategies to cope with many of the difficulties that arise in adult language classes, and look at key factors at all stages of the course.

- Pre-enrolment course publicity to give a full picture of what is on offer.
- Enrolment advice and guidance to recruit learners on to an appropriate course.
- First class tactics to help the students feel good from the outset.
- Creating a group spirit.
- Strategies to improve communication and sustain motivation.
- Tactics to deal with specific common problems perceived by students and teachers.
- What to do if someone misses a class.

Over to you

Task 1   Reflect on your own experiences as a learner.
- Have you ever enrolled for a part-time course?
- Was it as you expected?
- Did you complete the course? If not, can you at this stage identify any of the factors which caused you to drop out?

Task 2   What reasons have students ever given you for dropping out of classes?
- Do you think they were telling the whole story?

Before the course starts

Chapter 2

This chapter focuses on what happens before the start of a course, and highlights the importance of providing clear, concise information to potential learners — information which could forestall some of the problems which cause people to drop out of classes. It also considers whose role this is within an organisation and how to ensure that everyone concerned shares the responsibility for getting it right.

When a course fails to match up to the learner's expectations, however misguided those expectations might be, problems occur. People are very likely to drop out of classes when they:

Course information

- set themselves unrealistic goals;
- have a false impression of what goes on in a language class;
- do not realise the time and commitment required to learn a language.

But if they were better informed and more aware of what the course was going to entail, their expectations and reality might match more closely, and the problems might occur less often.

Another common reason for discontented learners leaving a course is the fact that, quite simply, they are not in the right class and they should never have been enrolled there in the first place. In many instances, this too can be avoided with better information and advice before the start of the course.

It is worth investing considerable effort into pre-course information. Its purpose is to:

- provide details of the course;
- ensure learners enrol on the appropriate course;
- prepare them for the course;
- dispel any wrong impressions.

It can be presented in various ways:

- in written form — prospectuses, leaflets, brochures, posters, adverts;
- on computer — some colleges have course information on computer terminals at various strategic points;
- by word of mouth — information given by tutors, careers officers, course organisers, secretaries, the switchboard operator;
- by practical experience — open days, taster sessions;

. . . but whichever form it takes, it is essential that it is clear, accurate, detailed, and easily and widely available.

Who provides course information?

It is in everyone's interest to improve retention rates, therefore tutors and organisers should share the responsibility for providing good quality information.

Most colleges have a member of staff responsible for processing course information, and part-time tutors often have very little involvement with the decision making. However, since the tutor is in the best position to supply accurate information, course organisers and publicity officers are usually only too delighted to receive constructive suggestions and offers of help from them when compiling course publicity.

If, as tutors, we feel that current publicity gives a wrong impression of our course or if we have not been completely happy with the way the course has been described, it is in our interest to explain why and to offer a more accurate version since inadequate or poor information can adversely affect retention rates.

It is, however, of little use offering one's services a few days before the start of the course. Publicity material for September courses is generally put together as early as March or April.

What information is needed?

If we are setting out to offer the student as much information about the course as possible, the information we present must be:

- user-friendly;
- clear and concise;
- detailed and accurate.

This is true whether the information is presented in a leaflet, passed over the phone by the Centre Head or an admissions secretary, or given by a guide during an open day.

Written information is generally produced in several formats, depending on the space available:

- detailed — all the course particulars, held centrally, and usually also on database;
- condensed — leaflets which might refer to all the language courses on offer;
- brief summary — advertisements in newspapers.

The time and effort put into compiling accurate course information is well rewarded. This is not only for learners' benefit. The course tutor, who may know everything there is to know about a class, will not necessarily be the person giving out the information. If someone rings up the college asking about the Italian course on Thursday evening, and there is no linguist present, the written information will probably be the only guide to the course. It must therefore be good enough for a non-linguist to be able to provide the necessary details. If the information given out is incorrect, insufficient or garbled, it is the tutor who is landed with the ensuing problem.

All the information needed about a course can be fitted comfortably on one A4 sheet as in the example shown on p14.

ITALIAN CLASS

TIME: WED/THURS EVENINGS FROM 6.30 pm

COURSE: BASIC GNVQ

LEVEL: QUITE EASY REALLY

EXAMS: NONE, EXCEPT AT END OF MODULE

PAYMENT: YES PLEASE

	Length

If it is a 30-week course, is this clearly stated? If it is advertised for ten weeks, does it end after the ten weeks or is there a follow on course? Is it assumed or hoped that students will stay for longer than ten weeks? Is it modularised?

	Cost

Is the stated cost for the whole course or for the first term only? Does it include examination fees? Can it be paid in instalments? Are there any concessionary rates? Is there a tax rebate?

Language/level	GERMAN I	Course number LN34G/96/E
Day/time	Monday 19.00–21.00	
Centre	Grange Adult Centre	
Course length	60 hours (2x30 weeks)	Start date 16/09/96
Entry requirements	None (course for complete beginners)	
Enrolment	At or before start of course. Later by agreement only.	Grange site 9–11/09/96 Main campus from 15/08/96
Course content ● Interaction — speaking and listening. ● Communicating very simply in predictable day to day situations. ● Basic structures of German.	Foundation course	
Learning outcomes In German . . . ● exchanging basic information about self, family, home and work; ● coping with public transport; ● finding one's way around; ● coping in a shop, restaurant, hotel reception, bank.		Cheshire European Languages Programme Level 1
Accreditation	NEAB	
Assessment	Continuous	
Progression	Level 2	
Cost	£68 incl. accreditation fee	
Books/materials	Approx. cost £10	not needed before start of course
Further information	Student services Tel: 00 000 000	

To be useful, this information needs to be detailed. If courses are organised in levels, a summary of what each level entails is necessary. The term Level 3 is only meaningful in the context of Level 2 and Level 4. Similarly, descriptors such as Intermediate or Advanced are of little use without further clarification as they can cover such a range of ability. Descriptors such as Improvers are meaningless.

It can help to include a 'bench mark', and as the only bench mark many people have ever heard of is GCSE, it may be helpful to refer to this or to other terms such as 'rusty 'O' level'. Many centres find it useful to list their courses as Year 1, Year 2, etc.

Level

A beginner's course would appear to have no entry requirements, but, in fact, it is very desirable that only complete beginners enrol at this level.

Entry requirements/ prior learning

When are the official enrolment sessions? What if someone misses these sessions? Is it possible to enrol at the first lesson? Can students enrol at any stage of the course or is there a cut off point? Is it necessary for late enrollers to have an interview with the course tutor?

Enrolment procedures

What will students be able to do by the end of the course?

Course outcomes

If the course concentrates on speaking and listening skills, it should be stated that the student will play an active part. Nobody will then be in a position to complain, *I didn't think I'd have to say anything.*

The nature of the course/course content

Is it assessed continuously? Is there an examination? Is it expected that everyone will participate in assessment? Who is the accrediting body?

Assessment and accreditation

Has the coursebook been selected? What is the approximate cost of any books or cassettes definitely to be used for the course?

Books/materials

Is there a college policy? Is there a minimum number of students needed for a class to run? In the case of popular languages, is it simply 'first come, first served' for the first twenty?

Minimum and maximum numbers

> ### Guidelines for course information
>
> For maximum effect . . .
>
> - Use a good layout and clear headings.
> - Be clear but concise — nobody wants to wade through a mass of prose to find the information.
> - Avoid specialist terms. Although the phrases 'communicative methodology' or 'non-Schedule 2' make instant sense to language teachers, they will mean nothing to most other people.
> - If you must employ some technical terms, explain what you mean by them; e.g. if you use the terms 'vocational' and 'non-vocational', explain that in broad terms the former involves assessment and accreditation and the latter has less emphasis on accreditation but might still involve some form of assessment.
> - Don't skimp on details of level and content.
> - When details of all the language courses have been compiled, put all the A4 sheets into a file (and/or on computer).
> - Ensure that there is a number to ring for further details and, whenever possible, a named person.
> - **Make sure that everyone who is remotely likely to be asked for information knows this is available and has access to it.**

You can take a horse to water . . .

However carefully the information may have been phrased, however detailed and eye-catching it is, there is absolutely no guarantee that it will be read. If the timid student with the rusty 'A' level in French has decided that he might like to start again as a complete beginner, he probably won't bother reading our plea for him to select the appropriate level. Do any of us bother with instructions when we think we know what to do?

Enrolment

The second stage of the pre-course information and advice process is enrolment. This is the time to make sure that all potential students . . .

- know as much as possible about the courses on offer;
- are enrolling at the right level.

It is also the time to look out for people who have not yet seen or sought any information about the courses.

The presence of a linguist is essential at enrolment. In fact, it is in all tutors' best interests to be present if at all possible. Even those who have not been asked to help will undoubtedly be welcomed with open arms if they offer to come along.

The enrolment period is usually a hectic time — queues of people waiting to be seen, pressure to fill in the relevant forms, complete the lists and get the paperwork over and done with. But concerted effort here goes a long way towards ensuring better classes. The aim is not simply to enrol people but to enrol them in the right class.

In an ideal world, publicity will have been circulated widely about the courses, all course descriptions are at hand, and it is only a matter of matching students to the right level. In reality, we can meet all sorts of obstacles to this seemingly straightforward procedure.

However delicate the task of changing their mind, it will be worth it. In what would obviously be the wrong class, there is a high prospect of these learners dropping out. There is an even higher prospect of them causing a lot of other people to drop out. A false beginner can be happily unaware of the devastating effect he is having on the confidence of true beginners. The person enrolled on too high a level can be similarly unaware that he alone is responsible for slowing the pace of the class for everyone else.

It is not always possible to have lengthy interviews with everybody who needs them. Students sometimes come to college when there is no linguist present to give advice and guidance. In such cases, it is imperative that there is some means of guiding them on to the correct level of competence. A simple chart, like the one illustrated on the following page, can be very effective in helping people decide for themselves which level would be most appropriate.

Self-diagnosis

NOT SURE WHETHER TO ENROL AT LEVEL 3?

Have you . . .

- completed a Level 2 course in this college, or a similar post-beginners' course elsewhere?
- studied the language to 'O' level/GCSE/RSA Stage I or equivalent (possibly many years ago)?
- used the language regularly and with some success on holiday or business in the foreign country?

YES

Read the Level 2 summary.

Can you, in the foreign language, do most of what is required? (Please be as objective as possible.)

NO → Consider enrolment at Level 2. Seek advice.

YES

Read the Level 3 summary.

Can you, in the foreign language, do most of what is required? (Please be as objective as possible.)

NO → Enrol at Level 3.

YES → Consider enrolment at Level 4. Seek advice.

Pressure to recruit

A major concern before the start of a course is whether there will be enough students for the course to run. Many colleges have a policy of twelve to fifteen as a minimum number for vocational courses. It is a good idea to advertise this policy prominently to avoid disgruntled students being surprised and disappointed at the cancellation of a class which has recruited five or six students.

There is considerable pressure on staff at enrolment to recruit the required number of students or risk not having a class, especially in the case of less commonly taught languages or higher level classes. But it is better to be open about the problem than to recruit anyone who happens to be passing. If a class fails to enrol enough people, there are not many options open.

- The first is for the class not to run. This is far from satisfactory and extremely disappointing for those who have enrolled.
- In large colleges with several centres, the learners can be offered a parallel course at another centre.
- Where a language laboratory is available, classes can be merged and the course then incorporates a flexible learning/self access dimension. Several small groups work in the language centre at the same time and meet as a group with a tutor less frequently than anticipated. Where the groups are learning the same language, this can be done without the use of a language laboratory through group work.

Because of the last minute nature of such decisions, they tend not to be immediately popular with students or tutor and can start the course off on a poor footing. However, the answer once again lies in adequate information and discussion. When students are actually involved in the discussions about the class, and it is made perfectly clear that it will incorporate a large element of self-access or that two small groups from two different centres must merge to be viable, they are prepared for the situation and more likely to rally round and respond to the challenge. It often happens that classes recruited on this basis have excellent retention rates.

To summarise . . .

Enrolment guidelines

- explain clearly all aspects of the course;
- don't assume that people have all the necessary information;
- answer questions fully;
- resist the temptation to gloss over the commitment and the time it takes to learn a language simply in order to recruit. It is hardly worth it if they are going to disappear within a few weeks.

Over to you

Task 1

Ensure that you are familiar with the pre-course information for the course(s) you teach. Consider whether it:

- is accurate enough;
- is detailed enough;
- successfully reflects what your class is about.

Task 2

Make a list of everything you would like potential students to know about your class(es).

First impressions

Chapter 3

Impressions gained at the first class will set the standard for the rest of the course and students who go home feeling uncomfortable about it may well be the first to drop out. It is probably the most important session of the whole course, and certainly the one we need to hold most tightly by the reins. Yet experience tells us that those first two hours often race by in a barely-controlled whirl of interruptions, administrative problems and late arrivals.

In this chapter we consider how to overcome such hurdles and ensure that students' first impressions of the class are favourable. We look at:

- planning that all important first class;
- welcome and induction to the college, to language learning and to the course;
- appropriate linguistic objectives;
- the importance of creating a group;
- ensuring flexibility.

The first session can be looked upon as a microcosm of the course as a whole, and as such will be judged by the same criteria. Both during the class and after it, students will be asking themselves, consciously or unconsciously, two questions:

If the answer to both these questions is 'Yes', then the students will be enjoying themselves and there is less chance of losing them.

Planning

> In planning the first session, the primary aims therefore will be:
>
> ● to ensure that the students feel as comfortable as possible;
> ● to ensure they leave the class being able to say something in the target language that they couldn't manage at the start.

The aims can be achieved by remembering to build in to the plan some well-known strategies.

● **Using ice-breaking activities** which mix the group up and help students and tutor to get to know each other.
● **Combining a variety of whole class, small group and paired activities** with no one task continuing for too long. That way, students will not become entrenched in a relationship with a single partner, latecomers will not feel excluded and any interruptions will not throw the plan too badly.
● **Presenting new language in small 'bites',** since it is less daunting in small steps and more easily achievable.
● **Building on what the students already know,** which is a great confidence booster. In the case of Level 2 students and upwards, it is a good idea for the tutor to start with some basics learnt in previous years. Beginners can be encouraged to focus on target language words in common use in English, phrases picked up on holiday, words relating to food and drink or fashion, art, music, places, politics . . .

Arriving at the first class

Even the most experienced tutors are nervous at the start of a new course.

Have I pitched the level of the course appropriately, or will there be some who can't cope?

Will there be enough students to run the course?

Will there be a good mix?

What will they be like?

Will I have any difficult characters this year?

These are all questions tutors ask themselves on the way to the first class. Imagine then the queries running through the minds of the new students as they make their way to that first meeting. It is well worth making a point of asking them how they felt about coming. Most will admit to being rather nervous and anxious and it will release some of the tension if the students understand that these sentiments are shared by everyone and are quite normal.

We all know how important it is to arrive in good time, so that the resources required and the lay-out of the room can be organised before the new students come in. That way the tutor is free to give a welcome to all as they arrive, check that everyone has come to the right place and, most importantly of all, will have spared the first arrival that heart-sinking experience of coming to a dark and empty room.

Some students, having enrolled earlier on a wave of enthusiasm, may well be having second thoughts when making their way to the first class. It is surprising just how many are frightened and apprehensive and have had to pluck up all their courage to come along. A friendly word of encouragement on arrival will do much to allay their fears.

The clear starting point is for tutors to introduce themselves. This is important not only for the obvious reasons but also because it immediately starts to build a relationship between tutor and students; a relationship which is often the lynchpin in maintaining good attendance. Students who feel no personal involvement with the tutor or with the rest of the group will find dropping out much easier, as they will imagine that no one will notice or care if they do not turn up.

Introductions

Students need to know the tutor's name and also a telephone contact number, to open up a channel of communication with the tutor from the beginning. This is the time to establish the ground rules for the course, to impress on the students that they are expected to let the tutor or someone at the centre know if they cannot attend a class.

Having a telephone number will also stand the students in good stead if they find there is a problem they would like to discuss but are unhappy to talk about it with others present.

Students also need to be introduced, to the tutor and to each other, and this is the next major step in creating relationships. However, at the early stage of the first session, while some of them might still feel a little nervous, it seems unnecessary to impose on them the traditional and nerve racking process of going round the class asking each one to introduce themselves in turn. As we see later in the chapter, there are more challenging and enjoyable ways of getting to know one another. Simply calling the names from the register of enrolments will be enough to help the tutor start to fit names to faces and does not put too much pressure on individuals.

Induction

At the first session there is always a great deal of information to pass on to the students — about the college's procedures and systems, about the facilities available to the students, the whole concept of language learning and the details of the course itself.

Induction to the college

Many colleges have specific induction programmes and provide a checklist to help the tutor deliver it. When well presented, it can be a valuable opportunity to make the students feel welcome and at home. Although some of them will be 'regulars', well-versed in the college's administrative and operational procedures, others will not have stepped inside an educational establishment since they left school twenty or thirty years before.

If the college's standard procedure is long and detailed, some of the information can be held over till the following session, since there are other, more pressing induction matters to be communicated on that first meeting.

Induction to language learning

We looked in Chapter 1 at some of the pre-conceived ideas and attitudes about learning brought to the classes by the students, and how a mis-match between expectations and actual experience can be one of the causes of drop-out. It follows then that some explanation and guidance at an early stage about the methodology used in class and some hints about study skills for language learning at home would help to prevent such misunderstandings.

There is a chance here to explain that tutor and student alike share the responsibility for successful learning, clearly setting out the two different roles in what is essentially a partnership of equals.

The tutor's responsibilities	The learner's responsibilities
• plan lessons; • present new language; • provide plenty of opportunity for practice and revision.	• take an active role; • make the most of opportunities in class; • make time in between classes to consolidate.

This shared responsibility can be a stumbling block if not fully understood, but a real bonus when students take it seriously. They are less likely to become disillusioned and to drop out later on if they understand the need to participate wholeheartedly.

Discussing tactics at the outset will ensure that all the players are aiming for the same goal and playing the same game! However, with so much to concentrate on in this first session, it is unrealistic to expect students to remember all they are told. A useful way of ensuring that they do remember their responsibility is to provide them with a simple leaflet, such as the one illustrated opposite, with some hints on effective language learning.

Guidelines for language learning

It can be presented and discussed at the first session and provides an opportunity for students and tutor to share their theories and experiences about the techniques that work. There may well be in the class a number of students who have had recent experience of the validity of such techniques. They are the tutor's most precious allies, and can be pressed to elaborate on what worked for them. For the new students, they are proof positive of what can be achieved.

Induction to the course
It is essential during this first session to share with the students some information about the course as a whole — the overall aims and rationale, and the specific language objectives.

- What are they aiming to achieve by the end of the course?
- Does the course focus in a balanced way on all four language skills, or does it concentrate more on some than on others?
- Is the syllabus based around topics, situations, language functions, or structures?

To make the most of your language course, remember the following . . .

- Learning a new language takes time. Be realistic in your expectations - don't expect to be fluent overnight.

- Don't worry about making mistakes. It is a normal part of the learning process. You will learn much more quickly if you try and express yourself, even though you may make a few mistakes, than if you say nothing until you are word perfect.

- Practise regularly. Unless you use and review what you have learnt you will forget it. Go over what you did in class frequently, as often as you can. And remember that twenty minutes a day is better than a mammoth session once a week.

- Say the words and phrases out loud when you practise. It is much more useful than reading them to yourself. Talk to anyone who will listen - to a fellow student, to yourself, to the cat! If you have a cassette recorder, record yourself.

- When learning words and phrases, use any method that works for you. Research shows that everyone's memory is different and you should stick to any method you trust. Do, however, keep an open mind and experiment with new ideas.

- Take an active part in your language learning and incorporate it into your daily life. Listen to cassettes in the car, make your shopping lists in the foreign language, watch television programmes about the foreign country - it all helps.

- Expect to understand more than you can say. This is quite normal.

  If you know you are going to have to miss a class, let your tutor know. S/he will then be able to let you know what the class will be covering that week and help you keep up at home.

- Relax. Don't compare yourself with others. People learn in different ways, at different speeds.

- Most important of all - enjoy yourself. Learning a language is extremely rewarding. This time next year we hope you will be delighted with the progress you have made.

- Is there an exam at the end of the course, or is assessment on a continuous basis?
- Is there a course book they should buy, or does the tutor provide all the materials required?

Most centres now base their language courses on discrete adult syllabuses, designed with reference to the National Language Standards, and generally set out in the form of course outcomes — what the students will be able to do in the target language by the end of the course. Although copies of these syllabuses should be available for students at enrolment, large numbers of students can still arrive at the class without having read them, or fully understood the contents. Some time spent explaining the objectives of the course will provide an opening for the students to explain their own motivation. Chapter 6 discusses the idea in more detail.

Students need to be given their own copy of the course outcomes, as these will be referred to often during the ensuing weeks to demonstrate progress and to motivate. It would be thoroughly off-putting to talk them through the entire contents at this stage, but they do need an explanation — some well chosen bullet points on the OHP might fit the bill, giving the tutor some pointers on which to expand during this opening presentation.

Creating relationships

The aim is that all the students in the class should start to get to know each other as quickly as possible. They will gel together as a group much more rapidly if given the opportunity of speaking to one another and of finding some common ground. Whilst each student's relationship with the tutor is important, their relationship with each other is equally so. It will be the promise of spending an evening with friends that will keep them coming, despite bad weather, pressure of work and other unforeseen hurdles. Chapter 4 looks in more detail at the group as a whole and the individuals within it.

Linguistic aims

So far then, much about induction, course objectives and building relationships, but didn't the students come to learn a language? As we have seen, there is so much to be accomplished during this first lesson that it could easily speed by with no actual target language being taught or learnt! It therefore makes sense to marry the social objectives with the linguistic ones by organising the 'getting to know each other' in the target language.

There are powerful psychological grounds for achieving the two ends with a common task. The students will feel much less inhibited when practising new language with new people if there is good reason for speaking. If the task they are trying to complete is important to them, they will focus much more on the actual message, the information being exchanged, than on the manner in which the exchange is taking place, i.e. the target language. Simply, if the students are keen to indulge their natural curiosity about the others in the group, they will be less inclined to be self-conscious about using strange new words and phrases.

Tutors commonly plan to concentrate on some aspect of personal identification at the first class, whatever the level. It is a useful way of enabling the students to find out more about each other, and it is a subject most people are happy to talk about. Whatever the language objectives set for this session though, during the practice phase, tutors should plan to give the students the opportunity of making contact with as many other members of the group as possible. Each small item of new language can be tried out on an ever-widening circle of the group, with the aim of helping the students to feel comfortable with each other.

Experienced tutors generally have an impressive armoury of ice-breaking activities at their disposal, most of which can be linguistically tailored to meet the needs of the moment. Three examples are set out below, designed to encourage practice in talking about oneself. These and the many other ideas to be found in the communicative activities books mentioned on p71 could all be adapted to encourage practice of other structures in different topic areas. But they would still retain that essential quality of an ice-breaking game — that of facilitating the maximum amount of social interaction.

Ideas for ice-breaking activities

1. Match the names to faces (Klippel, 1984)

Skills	Language	Level	Group	Materials
Speaking	Questions	Beginners	Whole class and tutor	A small slip of paper for each student

Each student and the tutor write their full name on a piece of paper. All the papers are collected, shuffled and redistributed so that all receive the name of a person they do not know. They then walk around the room trying to find the person whose name they have, by asking simple questions, e.g. *Is your name . . . . . . ? Are you . . . . ?* When everyone has found their partner, they introduce him/her to the group.

2. Identity cards (Klippel, 1984)

Skills	Language	Level	Group	Materials
Speaking Writing	Exchange of personal data	Any: depends on the cards prepared	Pairs, then small groups	A blank identity card for each student

Each student receives a blank identity card and is asked to interview a partner in order to complete the card with the partner's details. Cards can be very simple — *Name, Address, Nationality*, for beginners, or more complex — *Name, Family, Hobbies, Likes & Dislikes*, for higher level students. Once two students have interviewed each other, they then turn to another couple and take turns to introduce their partner to the others.

3. Find someone who . . . (Ur and Wright, 1992)

Skills	Language	Level	Group	Materials
Speaking	Exchange of personal data	Any: depends on the tasks set	Whole class and tutor	A copy for each student of a small list of criteria

Each student is given a short list of people to locate, e.g. Find someone who . . .
- was born in the same month as you;
- has the same number of brothers and sisters as you;
- who shares the same middle name as you;
- who drives the same car as you.

The criteria can be tailored to the specific language required, and to the level of the learners. Students must then circulate round the room, asking appropriate questions and noting down the names of those who fit the bill.

Before embarking on this type of activity, care must be taken to ensure that the students are well prepared linguistically for the exchanges required, with plenty of unthreatening choral repetition and practice before being expected to perform independently with unknown partners. However well-intentioned we might be to encourage learner autonomy, we are often over-eager to see our protégés perform in a 'meaningful, realistic exchange'! Fragile confidence is easily damaged by launching the students too quickly into an unsupported communicative activity. The student who feels embarrassed or unable to cope will retreat into his shell for the rest of the session — and might not even come back.

The types of tasks suggested to give much needed practice of new language have the added benefit of allowing the tutor to monitor and evaluate the students as they work. There is an opportunity here to begin to assess the confidence and competence of the new students. Later on, when the students have gone home, it is a good idea to jot down first impressions of each one. The notes will prove very useful later in the year when assessing their progress. However, whatever the level of the class, it is likely that at this first session there will be one or two students — or more — whose skills do not match those of the majority. The tutor has the perfect opportunity during the ice-breaker type activities to identify anyone in difficulty or who is plainly much stronger than the rest and is likely to be bored.

A word of warning!

Early diagnostic assessment

Students who find they have enrolled at the wrong level always need help and advice. Unless the tutor can identify the problem and suggest an appropriate move as quickly as possible, there is a risk of losing them. Most ill-placed students recognise straightaway that they feel uncomfortable and some will find an opportunity to talk to the tutor about it. Others, who are less brave, will simply not come again. It is important to try and have a quiet word with anyone who is obviously out of place and, if at all possible, to suggest alternatives. In small rural centres there may be no alternative class available. In this case the tutor should decide in consultation with the student on the appropriate course of action. There are many books written on the subject of mixed ability and differentiation which propose strategies to overcome the difficulties common in classes of mixed ability. Some useful ideas can be found in the books mentioned in the Further reading list on p71.

Where possible, suggest a transfer

Happily, in many colleges running large numbers of language classes, there is the possibility of proposing a move to a different level. This needs to be achieved as swiftly as possible, before the student has become too attached to the class, to his fellow-students and to the tutor, and also before a move to another class will make him feel like a 'new boy' trying to infiltrate a group of old friends. We are forever at pains to encourage flexibility in our students, trying to prevent them becoming too dependent on a particular approach or a particular partner. For our part we need to be equally as flexible, promoting the idea of transfers across the levels until each student has found the right niche. It can be tempting to hold on tightly to every class member, as insurance of meeting the magic number which makes for class viability. But we will surely lose before long a student who is wrongly placed, and it is a matter of professional pride that we are able to assess accurately the level of competence and find the right class for everyone wherever possible.

Relationships between tutors

Successful transfers are more easily made when the tutors know each other and their language programme well. Once a student has been identified as needing to transfer, it is fairly simple to phone the appropriate tutor and discuss it. Being forewarned about the arrival of new students, the colleague is able to greet them by name and introduce them to other members of the group. Moreover, the students feel they are being supported in a well-organised and cohesive system.

It might seem a daunting, or even impossible, task to keep in mind all these considerations and to cover all this ground at the first class, but they are all vital issues in our campaign to inspire our students and make them look forward to week two with impatience. Some of the general information about college systems and facilities can be held over till the next session and it is helpful to have the detailed information about college and the hints about language learning in written form for the students to take away and read at their leisure. Only so much can be taken in at once and the students should go home heads buzzing, not with documentation, but with new language.

But the class only lasts two hours!

To summarise the pointers to a successful first class:

- Prepare your lesson plan and materials well, so as not to be thrown by the unforeseen.
- Be warm, friendly and welcoming, inviting the students to drop their reserve.
- Give some information about the college or centre to make them feel at home.
- Talk with the students about language learning in general and your course in particular. Some tips about learning a language would be helpful, making it clear it doesn't happen overnight.
- Create as many opportunities as possible for students to work together and get to know each other.
- Make sure that the language you teach is:
  - presented in small steps so as not to be daunting;
  - well practised, in an unthreatening way;
  - and practised again, in a realistic interactive way, so the students can leave the class feeling they have acquired a useful skill.
- Listen out for students who are obviously much stronger or weaker than the rest. They may need guidance.

It is a fact that there is much to be achieved in this first session, but a well planned lesson gives confidence and more confidence comes with practice. Good language tutors are by nature 'multi-tasking' and are able to do many of these things without conscious effort. As experience grows, so do the radar-like properties which enable us to listen to two or three conversations at once and to home in on potential difficulties before they become problems.

Over to you

Task 1   Does your college or centre provide an induction checklist? If so, what do you feel are the most important elements to pass on to students at the first class?

Task 2   If you have no induction materials, what could you tell the students at your first meeting about college facilities and resources in order to make them feel more at home?

Task 3   Have you any other language-learning tips you have found useful to pass on to your students?

Task 4   Can you suggest any other ice-breaking activities which, in your experience, help to create a good atmosphere at the first session?

The group dynamic

Chapter 4

We saw in the previous chapter the need to encourage right from the start the development of good relationships within the group. These relationships are essential for the social cohesion of the group, but they are much more than that. There are educational and linguistic benefits deriving from a healthy group dynamic.

When we study the characteristics of our most successful classes, we find that they thrive and flourish, embracing new members too, because of an atmosphere of mutual support. This support network is not only a social one but is also important in terms of the learning that takes place, with the strong helping the weak, the confident encouraging the timid and, on a purely pragmatic level, the regulars supporting those who find it hard to attend every class.

Results from the Mid-Cheshire College survey of drop-outs revealed some evidence of students feeling isolated; distanced from the group whether in ability, confidence or in sheer practical terms by the impossibility of attending every session. They seemed to have failed to become integrated into the main body of the group. If that sense of isolation is avoided, then there is much more hope of the group remaining intact.

Each new group sets out on a course as a mixed bag of individuals, with differing abilities, motivating forces and expectations, but when the group starts to gel, there is a reaction which takes place, melting the hard edges of the individual members and resulting in an amalgam which is stronger and somehow much more than the sum of its parts.

It is the tutor's role to facilitate that type of reaction by the successful management of the group as a whole. This means knowing and understanding the students. In the early sessions it is of course impossible to know them well, but for an experienced tutor it is possible usually to recognise some typical behaviour patterns and therefore certain types of learner.

Mutual support

The melting pot

Typical characteristics

The shrinking violet

Timid and lacking in confidence. Sometimes this is just in the learning environment, or may be shy in life as a whole. Will certainly not want to be singled out or to address the whole class. Will look to the tutor for confirmation of every utterance.

The eager to please

Badly wants to shine. Values praise above all things and might even have enrolled at a lower level than is really suitable, in order to display knowledge. Can be soul-destroying to other members of the group.

The quietly confident

Happy to perform whenever requested. Knowledgeable and sensitive. Handles the new language with confidence and competence. A real asset.

The group leader

One of life's born organisers. May or may not be competent with new language, but never fails to be confident — sometimes very off-putting to the timid, but can be an asset when well-managed.

The veteran campaigner

Can be any age but has had much experience of adult language classes. Not always successful, but enrols year after year regardless. Knows the system.

Has tried language-learning before, probably at school some years ago and was found wanting. Convinced of being useless at languages. Needs praise to boost confidence.

The battered ego

Might have learned to read and write the language at school long ago, but dare not speak for fear of making a false utterance. Feels the need to prepare everything in writing before answering a question. Likes to display knowledge of grammar. Can be off-putting to those who have none.

The grammarian

Feels the need to know and understand the origins of all new language before using it. Sometimes confused with the grammarian, but simply more interested in etymology. Either way disrupts the class by destroying the pace of the lesson.

The persistent questioner

Might own or have access to a house or apartment in the country of the target language. Has a wealth of knowledge about the systems and a wide range of every day vocabulary but often fossilised English accent. Very helpful when sharing enthusiasm and as a source of authentic materials.

The semi-permanent resident

Has travelled far and wide, often towing a caravan. Many anecdotes to tell about mishaps and incidents. Useful in persuading the others of the need to learn the language.

The seasoned traveller

Mixed-ability

Taking care to ensure that students receive advice and guidance at enrolment can help them to enrol at the right level. Careful monitoring during the first session can enable tutors who still find students who are obviously too weak or too strong for the class to suggest alternatives. But even within each level, it would be rare indeed to find an adult language class which does not include learners of a very wide range of ability, experience and background.

Susan Ainslie, in *Mixed-ability teaching: meeting learners' needs* (1994), identifies the following key areas of 'mixed-ability':

● motivation, interests and needs;
● linguistic ability;
● general educational background;
● learning style;
● age;
● external pressures and time available to study;
● anxiety.

All these factors, plus the stereotypical characteristics we mentioned before, will influence how comfortable the students are in the classroom and therefore their ability to learn the language. Experienced tutors will recognise the value of being aware of all these influences and will adopt strategies to minimise any destructive impact. Indeed, the tutor who is effectively managing the group will be exploiting all these differences with beneficial results.

Well chosen pairs and small groups can do much to boost the confidence of the shrinking violet, can give a role to the born organiser, can exploit the experience of the veteran campaigner and can put the knowledge of the grammarian to good use. It may take time to find just the right mix of talents, but while the tutor is trying out various permutations, the new students are gradually getting to know other members of the group and growing in confidence. Moreover, it is actually preferable to encourage frequent changes of partners in class activities, as the students are likely to gain much from the happy combinations and, if they are regularly moved on, will have less time to suffer in an unsuitable group.

Tutors will understand that it is not possible to give hard and fast rules as to who might successfully work with whom. Whilst we can illustrate here the concept of symbiotic groupings, giving an indication of the experiences which have shaped some of the characters involved, the success of these groups is wholly dependent on the awareness and experienced eye and ear of the tutor. It is evidence again of the tutor managing the individuals with the aim of creating a well-knit group.

The organisation of activities in large and small groups and in pairs has other benefits, too. Responsibility is devolved from tutor to learner and the learners have more control. They are often able to learn as much from each other as from the tutor and have more opportunity to speak and practise the language.

With sympathetic management then, it is possible to turn potentially divisive factors to the advantage of the group. If the tutor also goes on to exploit the natural talents and skills of the group members, there is even more to be gained.

Exploiting the skills available

Try as he might, the tutor is rarely a 'jack of all trades'. Many bemoan the fact that their artwork is so poor. Others have panic attacks at the mere thought of using a video machine or projector. These skills can of course be acquired, but it can be very comforting for the students to see that the tutor who is so confident with the target language, is obviously weaker in other areas.

It makes sense to capitalise on all the skills available. If a member of the group is a talented artist, then that student can be asked to draw symbols on the board, etc. If there is someone who enjoys singing and does not suffer from stage-fright, then that member could enliven the proceedings with a well-chosen song. The student who is very timid but obviously computer-literate could be the one to demonstrate the language program on the CD-ROM. And of course, when flummoxed by the apparent inertia of the television and video equipment, we should request the services of an expert, for there is bound to be one.

In the same way, the class can be a forum for sharing the adventures of the students and tutor on visits abroad, or on meeting native speakers. There are few people who have not at some time been surprised, misled or downright frightened by something they have witnessed or experienced and the group framework makes the perfect platform for discussion of these incidents, with a view to forewarning others. Banking problems, curious customs, points of etiquette which differ from ours, are all topics which can be usefully aired and discussion of them will help unite the group in a feeling of common ownership.

The creation of a shared library of foreign language newspapers, magazines and tourist office brochures is another tactic tutors can employ to encourage interdependence and a collective spirit. All students love to browse through such materials and it is easy to see how much more variety can be enjoyed when all these resources are shared — and of course it links the students with a common interest which is not dependent on language competence.

Once pooled in this way, the telling of stories, the deployment of skills and the sharing of authentic materials within the group are powerful levellers, activating the skills of 'tutor' in all the group members and reinforcing their value as part of the team. The tutor cannot be all things to all people, but as long as the group has confidence that the tutor's knowledge of the target language is sound and as long as they understand the rationale behind the methodology adopted, then they will respect the tutor for those things and take up the baton themselves in other areas.

Activities beyond the syllabus

So far, we have looked at the fostering of a strong group dynamic while actually delivering the syllabus, when students are working towards their linguistic objectives. But our students are adults and their aims in enrolling on the course may not be purely linguistic ones. *No educational group, however objective its context or purpose might be, is solely held together by its learning-related purpose.* (Hotho Jackson, 1995)

There is often a hidden social agenda which the tutor can exploit to great advantage. Film and theatre trips, restaurant meals and even coffee and croissant breaks in the classroom, all help the students to see each other and the tutor in a different light and break down the barriers caused by preconceived notions of confidence, competence and role. Such activities are enjoyable in their own right, but if the theme of them is linked with some aspect of the culture or tradition of the target language country, then they also help to present the language in a more holistic way. The students will not be learning in a vacuum and their motivation will be increased. In our small way we shall be emulating the conditions which favour language acquisition: we shall be bringing the country into the classroom and taking the students out in search of the real country. Students who are involved in this way have strong incentives to complete the course.

Below are illustrated some suggestions for possible social activities. The organisation of these events need not always be left to the tutor. Members of the class are often willing to take on the role of social secretary, creating yet more links and networks within the group. Moreover, the events themselves can be a major factor in maintaining or even rekindling the motivation of students who are starting to find the language learning more difficult than they expected.

BEYOND THE PROGRAMME: IDEAS FOR SOCIAL ACTIVITIES

 Cinema and theatre trips

 Meals out

 Quizzes

 Films in the classroom

 Presentations or talks about past holidays

 Befriending the EFL students

 Getting together with other groups

 End of terms eats and drinks

 Correspondence with students of English, from a twin town perhaps

 Sharing tourist office materials

 Visits to exhibitions

Over to you

Task 1

Think about the different characters in classes you have taught.

- Drawing on your own experience, can you add to the 'types' listed on pp34–35?
- Can you describe the characters in a grouping which worked particularly well?
- Have you had experience of a group which was less successful? Can you think why that was?
- What other skills might students be able to offer which could be helpful in class and encourage a feeling of interdependence?
- Have you been able to bring the country to the students with social and cultural activities? What type of events have they and you found enjoyable?

Maintaining motivation

Chapter 5

If all has gone according to plan during the initial stages of the course, the majority of the students will be in the appropriate class, aware of their objectives, their commitment and the nature of the course, and hopefully stimulated by their achievement in the first few lessons.

Having got off to a good start and having set the standard, we are faced with the challenge of living up to it for the next 26 weeks or so! We must continue to ask ourselves:

because these two questions are as relevant for every lesson as they are for the first.

Schemes of work

A good course is made up of many elements: syllabus, materials, activities, atmosphere, interaction, group dynamic and even accommodation contribute to the overall success.

The syllabus, which provides the framework for the course and defines the content, is generally decided at institution level. The focus of this chapter is on how the syllabus is delivered and how it can best be done to maintain learner motivation. Since most tutors are now required to provide details in advance of how they intend to deliver their course, we start with the scheme of work.

A scheme of work is an overall plan of how the course is to be delivered, providing the details of how learners will be guided through the syllabus to achieve the course objectives.

Whether the format of the scheme of work is at the discretion of the tutor or produced to a prescribed formula, its essential purpose is to lead tutors to think through such issues as:

- what they intend to cover;
- how they intend to do this;
- the order in which topics will be presented;
- how and when assessment will be integrated;
- what materials to use;
- what activities to use;
- how to integrate cultural and linguistic objectives;
- when to integrate 'beyond the syllabus' activities;

. . . in other words, to have a clear overview of the whole course.

Having a scheme of work ensures a structured approach and prevents panic at the end of the course when it is realised that much of the syllabus has been overlooked and several assessments are outstanding. During inspections, schemes of work are required as proof that the tutor and the centre have an overall perspective of the course and that each lesson is part of a planned progression and not simply a haphazard event.

However, care must be taken not to allow the scheme of work to become a straitjacket preventing a tutor from responding to learners' immediate needs. The most useful schemes of work are working documents which allow for creative thinking while still ensuring a structure to the course.

The elements of a course which hinge on social interaction, such as atmosphere and relationships, have been discussed in previous chapters. But before moving on to consider which materials and approaches are more likely to motivate learners, we reflect briefly on one particular aspect of the relationship between tutor and learners — that of trust.

Inspiring trust and confidence from the start

Learners need to trust the tutor — professionally as well as personally. They must be confident that we know what we are talking about if they are to gain the most from the lessons. Although respect is something a tutor has to earn over a period of time and there are no real short cuts to this, there are ways of helping to ensure that learners have confidence in our professional competence.

- The first step in the process may well be to ask the students outright to place their trust in our knowledge of language learning.

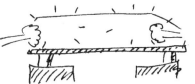

*Materials and
activities which
motivate*

- This can be reinforced by regular explanations of the principles of language learning — repetition, reinforcement, saying things out loud — so that learners always understand why they are being asked to do something or why we have chosen a particular activity.
- We can invite feedback from learners, so that they are given the opportunity to tell us what they like and don't like about the materials and activities used. There are suggestions for organising the feedback in Chapter 6, and the information gained can reveal fascinating insights into the way learners perceive the class and into language learning in general. It can also guide our methods and ensure that we remember to explain why it is necessary to do something which might not be entirely popular.

The materials and activities we use obviously play a major part in motivating learners. What constitutes successful learning materials and activities? Do some motivate more than others? If so, why? What are the elements that make people respond positively, leading them to enjoy the learning process and stay with the course?

In this section we present our criteria for successful materials and activities for the adult language class, based on our own experience and on our collaboration with many other tutors. We make no apologies that some of them are obvious, since it is often easy to overlook the obvious. There will also be occasions when a tutor has good reason to choose materials which conform to none of the criteria — but this is definitely an occasion to explain those reasons!

Materials which motivate are:

- **consistently interesting, and of specific interest to adults,** so it is a good idea to steer clear of materials written for thirteen-year-olds. Paradoxically, some materials written for young children, which would be anathema to the adolescent, can be used successfully with adults.
- **up to date,** involving the use of current language, topical words and phrases and idiom. Dated textbooks where the photographs, prices and realia bear little ressemblance to present day reality generally find little favour with learners, especially if the whole course is based on such a book.
- **designed to foster interaction** wherever possible, since people tend to learn best through activity and participation. Arguably the most

important resource of the adult classroom is the adult learner who is generally a willing participant in the kind of communicative activities which encourage speaking skills and foster the social element so important to retain learners.

- **challenging but not too difficult** — every activity must be within the learner's ability and allow success. Although we should be aiming to stretch and challenge learners, it is better to err on the side of caution when deciding if an activity is manageable. The confidence generated by success will make up for the fact that the activity is over too quickly. Materials inducing a regular sense of failure, on the other hand, are guaranteed to demotivate.
- **appropriate to the level of the course.** Using a coursebook which is too difficult or unnecessarily complex can lead to demotivation. Nothing is more discouraging than to be still struggling to complete Unit 1 in late November.
- **enjoyable.** To keep our learners we have the responsibility of ensuring not only that the course fulfils its learning purpose but that is does so in an enjoyable way.
- **varied.** We should remember that learners in evening classes may be tired after a day's work, and may have trouble concentrating. Concentration will be enhanced by a variety of short activities, rather than by two hours devoted to one or two long ones.

When planning a variety of activities to present and practise language, there are three elements which can be mixed and matched to provide a very large number of combinations. The columns opposite illustrate some of the possibilities.

One or more items selected from each column will create a wide variety of possibilities with which to sustain the interest of the group whilst carrying out practical tasks and ensuring plenty of opportunity for practice. It does make sense to limit the use of activities which require no interaction, such as individual written exercises. The learner can do these at home.

There are many excellent books available on the subject of producing teaching materials. The NETWORD series and the Pathfinder series from CILT abound with good ideas and it is surprising how one good idea leads to another and can inspire a whole streak of creativity. For more detail, see the Further reading list on p71.

Resources	Activity	Group
OHP	games	whole class
audio tapes	role plays	large groups
tape recorder	surveys	small groups
video tapes	quizzes	pairs
camcorder	interviews	individuals
board	listening & responding	
paper & pen	reading & responding	
realia	information gap activities	
slides & projector	choral repetition	
photographs	discussions	
course book	songs/music	
language assistant		

Sharing ideas and materials   Another source of inspiration is to work with colleagues. Some colleges organise regular meetings of language tutors, where ideas and materials can be shared and problems and successes aired. The team spirit engendered by such meetings rarely fails to provide inspiration — getting together to share materials not only cuts down on workload but can generate a wealth of interesting hints and ideas. It can also highlight ideas which appear to be good but simply don't work in the classroom.

Unfortunately, in some centres there is no such support system and tutors have little opportunity to get to know each other, to share experiences, gripes and triumphs. There may, however, be a local NETWORD group. These groups are self-help groups of language tutors who meet within the NETWORD framework of support. Details of exisiting groups are available from CILT.

Coursebooks

Why should tutors bother at all with producing materials? Is there really a need to organise all the activities mentioned? Why not just follow a coursebook?

There is no shortage of coursebooks for adults on the market for French, German, Spanish and Italian, and comprehensive lists are available from CILT. There are also lists for other languages, but the range is more modest. Because it is a competitive market, these books are generally of a high standard. Despite this, one of the mysteries of teaching is that no tutor ever claims to have found the perfect coursebook. We all think that we can improve on them, presumably because teaching is such a subjective business and because all classes are different.

However, while we may feel that materials we have produced ourselves are more directly useful to our learners, we shouldn't forget that a good coursebook will have been carefully planned, written, edited and field tested. Most are beautifully produced to a quality we could not hope to match. They provide the support of audio (and sometimes video) cassettes and some have teachers' notes to assist lesson planning. For the learner they can provide a structure, a tangible means of confirming that progress is being made and an excellent means of revising.

There are two golden rules to remember about coursebooks.

1   They should be chosen with great care because once a tutor has asked the class to buy a particular book, however unsuitable it might turn out to be, learners are likely to be extremely reluctant to buy another.

Most publishers provide inspection copies which allows the time to judge which book will be most suitable for both tutor and learners. It is unwise to rely on publishers' catalogues for information! Make sure the book you have chosen is easily available.

2   Plodding mechanically, page by page, through the coursebook with the class is not particularly motivating. If this is all that is happening in the class, students could justifiably ask themselves after a few weeks whether it is worth bothering to attend at all when they could do the same thing at home by themselves.

A more stimulating alternative is to base the course on a book, using the dialogues, listening to the cassettes and exploiting the situations and the characters, and then to use the class contact hours to develop the material, to set up activities which the learners would not be able to do at home by themselves because they involve interaction.

The wealth of exercises and cultural information provided in the best books can be used:

- as a source of revision at the beginning of each lesson;
- as a means of building a profile of what has been learned which can feature in the learner's portfolio of evidence. Such a portfolio is often required as part of the assessment of the course;
- as a reference work providing useful back-up;
- to provide work for learners to do at home.

Homework

The vexed question of whether to set or not to set homework for adults in language classes is one that has taxed most tutors at some time. Whilst on the one hand, homework constitutes a concrete link tying one class to the next and helping students to see some progression in their language learning, it can be the very task that distances them from the group. How often have we heard students say that they felt reluctant to attend the class because they had not found time to complete the homework set?

A means must therefore be found of explaining to the students from the outset that they will not incur the tutor's wrath if they arrive without having done the work. In fact, when they come to the next class they will usually be able to benefit from a sharing of work carried out by other students.

Traditionally, language homework has often consisted of learning lists of vocabulary or of preparing written exercises to be handed in to and marked by the teacher. But it can be much more creative and stimulating than that, and in the language learning process work carried out by the students at their own pace at home can play one or more of the following important roles:

- **consolidation** — reinforcing what has been covered in class;
- **extension** — offering an opportunity for stronger students to display more of their talents than is sometimes possible given the constraints of mixed ability classes;
- **revision** — providing a context for a look back over a particular topic area, perhaps prior to carrying out an assessment task;
- **self-assessment** — encouraging the students to try their hand at a specific task and to evaluate how they coped with it;
- **preparation** — inviting the students to carry out work which will offer a lead-in to a new topic.

Homework set during, or at the end of, one session can be the point of departure of the next. In that way, it fulfils the need to set each class in the context of what has gone before and what is to come. Instead of merely handing homework in to the tutor for marking, the work completed can be shared in small groups and each person's contribution discussed. This practice will encourage self and peer evaluation of the work and has the added bonus of supporting those who did not find time to do it.

An early opportunity of looking at last week's work also provides a helpful prop — a pointer to those who were unable to attend the previous class. This is perhaps the moment to supply copies of any worksheets they missed and to suggest how they might best make up the lost ground. As can be seen in Chapter 7, practical help given to a student who has had to miss a class is essential for maintaining his commitment and motivation.

● Written homework which when shared with a small group requires all the students to listen and guess something.

Examples of effective homework activities

Year 2	Describing a famous family
Talking about one's family	Students prepare an anonymous description of a famous family, real or fictitious. They give details of: ● the sphere in which the family is so well known — politics, cinema, television, literature, etc; ● age and profession of parents; ·number and age of children; ● other relations important in that family. In small groups, students read their prepared descriptions. Other group members must guess the name of the family.

- Homework which entails preparing something to present to others in the group.

Year 2 upwards	Describing a successful holiday
Talking about the past	Students each select two photos from their favourite holiday. They prepare a few details to pass on to others in the group: ● where they went; ● what they did; ● what they saw; ● what the weather was like. Other students can then pose supplementary questions.

- Homework which requires the student to undertake some research.

Year 3	Comparing weather forecasts
Talking about the weather	Students are asked to find out the weather forecast for the day of the next class — from newspapers, radio or television. They prepare an outline of it in the target language to be presented to others in a small group. The forecasts from the different sources can be compared and evaluated for meteorological accuracy.

- Homework entailing reading and reporting back.

Year 1 upwards	Reading to glean new vocabulary
Any relevant topic	Students are asked to read a short passage, perhaps from the coursebook, on a theme related to that of the lesson. They are instructed to look up unknown words in the glossary. Half the students are asked to make a list of new verbs; the other half to make a list of new nouns. At the next class, the tutor makes small groups comprising some students with verbs and some with nouns. They combine resources to make sentences recreating the gist of the original text.

● Homework entailing practising and making a recording.

Year 1 upwards	**Giving & understanding directions in the street**
Making cassette recordings	Students are asked to practise their oral response to a question, perhaps a request for directions in the street. They then decide on a destination and record their directions to it from a map supplied by the teacher. In class, the recordings are played back in small groups and other students must follow the route on the map and pinpoint the destination. They might also wish to comment on each other's performance!

This last suggestion can prove extremely helpful when building up evidence of student competence for assessment and accreditation. Many awarding bodies require tutors to provide recorded evidence from each student and this is a time-consuming activity in class. What is more, having to perform 'live', into a microphone with an audience, can be utterly intimidating for even the most confident student. Asking the students to record their contributions at home does much to defuse this threatening situation and helps make the assessment process as painless as possible.

Assessment

Assessment involves more, of course, than requesting random recordings of students' performances. All language courses funded by the FEFC have to be accredited by a recognised awarding body, and many non-vocational courses funded by LEAs also involve assessment of learners' progress.

With the aims of ensuring the quality of the course, and demonstrating that it has identifiable learning goals which are being met, learners' progress is monitored and evaluated, and their achievement recorded. In the vast majority of cases this is organised by the tutors and involves them in:

● evaluating whether their learners have achieved the learning objectives of the course;
● providing evidence of their competence to the awarding body.

Assessment is a powerful motivating factor when handled sensitively and organised with the interests of learners paramount. It helps to give structure to a course and makes it easier to recognise and reward the learner's achievements.

However, if it is not handled well, it can result in problems and, at worst, could turn out to be one of the reasons for drop-out. It makes no sense to allow the very factor which was introduced to motivate and guarantee quality to alienate the learners from their language learning. Therefore we have to organise our assessment with great care — in Adult Education we cannot afford mistakes, we have to get it right first time.

Assessment schemes are not generally left to the individual tutor to organise, but are compiled by groups of tutors working together. It is a time consuming task, involving the need for clear ideas on the whole extent of the course:

- the learning objectives;
- assessment materials and activities;
- the process of recording evidence;
- classroom management;
- moderation;

. . . and the process should be thought through as a whole from start to finish before it is implemented. One could devise the apparently perfect assessment scheme, conforming to the most rigorous academic criteria, with faultless paperwork . . . but if students shun it and vote with their feet, it is valueless. If we are spending more time assessing than teaching and we are constantly struggling with paperwork to the detriment of teaching, then the balance is wrong.

The book *Assessing adult learners* (1995) deals in some detail with assessment, and the following is only a brief summary of the factors to bear in mind if assessment is to motivate learners to stay the course rather than cause them to abandon it.

- The way assessment is presented to learners can make all the difference to its successful implementation. It should be introduced as an integral part of learning a language right from the beginning of the course, and the advantages highlighted.
- Assessment need never be a threatening, intimidating process. If it does cause anxiety and stress to learners, not only will they not show their true competence, but they may well not bother to turn up again.
- The balance of the course must be right. If learners feel that assessment has taken over, and that the tutor is more interested in filling the tick-sheet than in them, they are justified in being dissatisfied with the course.

- The materials and activities used should follow the same principles and conform to the same criteria as good teaching materials. They should be challenging and enjoyable, motivating the learners and allowing them to demonstrate what they have learnt.
- Developing the assessment materials and the paperwork necessary for recording achievement can be very time consuming, especially if produced by every individual tutor. It saves a lot of work and also acts as a useful moderation exercise if tutors work together.
- When first deciding on the evidence of competence to be submitted to the awarding body it is vital to think the whole process through and agree on evidence which is feasible to collate while still maintaining standards. Problems result if collecting the agreed evidence turns out to be unrealistic and impractical in the classroom.

The quality of a course is apparent when students persevere with their course, enjoy their classes and make good progress. Assessment is about quantifying and demonstrating this quality, not about changing the essential nature of the course.

Self assessment

The above tends to convey the impression that assessment is the sole concern of the tutor. But it concerns first and foremost the learner, and introducing them to the concept of self-assessment is a way of encouraging them to develop ownership of their learning. The more involved they become with their learning, the less likely they are to abandon the course. This is the theme of the next chapter.

Over to you

Task 1

How many elements can you add to the table of Resources/Activities/Groups on p44.

Task 2

How many different combinations can you make from the final list?

Task 3

Using the table as a guide, list under the following headings the resources, activities and materials you use.

Regularly	Occasionally	Never

Task 4

Does the system of assessment you use suit you and the class?
    If so, list the good points.
    If not, identify what is wrong with it.

Learner autonomy

Chapter 6

Much has been written about learner autonomy and its place in language learning today (see Further reading, p71). We consider it here in the context of motivating adult learners, and define it in its widest sense as **the acceptance of responsibility by the learner for his or her own learning.** It is not another name for self-study, nor a method of dispensing with the tutor, and although it clearly implies independence, there is nothing contradictory between the concept of learner autonomy and that of a strong group dynamic.

Learners actively involved in their course, who feel a sense of ownership for their learning, will be less willing to abandon that course than learners who feel that the course is the responsibility of the tutor or the college, and who imagine that their sole contribution is to turn up to the lesson.

The process of transferring control and responsibility for learning to the learner is a strand which runs through all stages of the course. The key is **involvement**, and the principal means we have of involving the learner are:

- information;
- negotiation;
- evaluation;
- feedback.

The first stage is to provide the learner with accurate and adequate information about the course itself and about the process of learning a language. Chapters 2 and 3 indicate the kind of information which is useful, and highlight the importance of sharing this information right from the beginning of the course. The first session is the time to present the notion of a shared responsibility for learning, to state clearly that it is a two way process, and to highlight the contribution expected from learners if they are to make the most of their course (see p25).

Information

Negotiation

An essential component of the information learners need is a set of clear objectives for the course, which need to be agreed at the first session. Agreement is essential if the goals are to be seen as the learner's and not the tutor's. Although a vocational course designed to fulfil the requirements of a specific accrediting body is of necessity tightly defined, no course should be so rigid that it does not leave room for some negotiation with the students, if only to decide on the weight of emphasis on a particular topic.

Presenting the course objectives as suggested on p14 provides an opening for students to explain their reasons for enrolling. While some may not have clearly formulated reasons or may have difficulty in articulating their motives, others will know very clearly what they would like to be able to do.

> I'd love to be able to chat to my son's Italian in-laws.

> I want to be able to cope with the unforeseen on holiday.

> I need to understand what my opposite number in Spain is saying to his colleagues in meetings.

If the course is well designed and focused on adults' needs, it is unlikely that the tutor will have any difficulty pointing out how the intended programme will marry with the students' individual requirements. Where necessary, the programme can be adapted to take into account some of the suggestions made. There is little point spending weeks learning to cope in French with every possible aspect of rail travel if the students are unanimous in their intention of getting about France by car.

This element of negotiation will help the students to feel they have a stake in the learning process, that their views are being sought and that their particular needs are being met.

The negotiation process is of course a compromise, but an open discussion on the subject usually reveals that the common needs are far more prevalent than the differing ones. Should the process uncover a student whose requirements are radically different from those of the rest of the class, then it could be that the class is not suited to this person and this would be the ideal time to suggest alternatives.

Care must be taken during the negotiation not to get carried away and to imply that there is no limit to what can be achieved during the course. There is an inherent danger that unless the tutor keeps a tight hold of the discussion, the learners will develop wildly unrealistic expectations which will inevitably leave them disillusioned before very long.

Realism

Evaluation

Having established the objectives and planned the course in such a way that they can be met, the tutor, as the year unfolds, will constantly be monitoring learners' progress towards these objectives.

However, it is not enough for the tutor to know that all is going according to plan — this must also be communicated to the learners. One of the most powerful sources of motivation is success, and tutors can sustain motivation by ensuring that learners are fully aware that they are achieving. Quantifying progress, whether it refers to a term's work or to a single activity, can be one of the most effective means of motivating learners and keeping them coming to the course.

Going one step further, learners should also be given every encouragement to evaluate for themselves the progress they are making towards their goals. They should be encouraged to form their own opinion of their progress rather than rely exclusively on the tutor's. Reflecting on their learning on a regular basis will:

Self evaluation

- spur them on by providing evidence of progress;
- help them to learn more effectively, by making them more aware of their strengths and weaknesses;
- reinforce the idea that they have a responsibility for their own learning;
- minimise their dependence on the tutor.

There is no set format, no right or wrong way of evaluating, and it can be achieved in a variety of ways. The following are examples of how it might be carried out.

Variety

- Overall progress against the course objectives can be discussed periodically, and learners invited to refer to the list and to tick off the goals they feel they have achieved, either wholly or in part. This need not take very long — ten minutes at the end of a session can send them home feeling very positive about their learning.

- Most good coursebooks set out the learning objectives, not only for the whole course but also for each unit. When a unit is completed, learners can check whether they can do what they are expected to be able to do. This can be in the form of a small group discussion or done individually at home. The set exercises are generally a good indicator of progress.
- The emphasis on competence based learning with its global 'can do' ethos can sometimes lead us to overlook detail, but it is often useful to ask learners to reflect on specific aspects of their language learning.
  — listening
  — speaking
  — reading
  — writing
  — vocabulary
  — pronunciation
  Learners can be asked to award themselves marks from 1 (unsatisfactory) to 5 (very good) for a particular aspect.
- If there is the possibility of occasional access to recording equipment, it can be a good opportunity to ask them to record a dialogue with a partner, listen to it and then evaluate their pronunciation.
- Quizzes can be an effective means of raising learners' awareness of any gaps in their knowledge. They can be used on a whole group, team or individual basis.

Support for learners

Although some people will be familiar with the notion of self evaluation, for some it will be a new concept and one which will need plenty of support from the tutor, particularly at the initial stages.

It is of necessity a very subjective process and dependent on a host of personal factors such as confidence or mood. First attempts might reveal learners' estimation of their achievements to be wildly inaccurate and unreliable. The criteria by which to judge progress in language learning are not easy to define precisely, especially at higher levels. We all know how difficult it can be to gauge the precise degree of sympathy expected from the sympathetic native speaker.

Some people will gloss over problem areas which need to be addressed, while others will be over critical of themselves.

> *. . . there is evidence that women tend to undervalue themselves and allocate themselves marks that are on average 10% lower than those allocated by their teacher.* (Brown and Knight, 1994)

All students therefore need to be guided to be as objective as possible, and in this they will take the lead from the tutor.

Every learner needs some positive feedback, even when there is clear room for improvement. The tutor should make sure they are evaluating against criteria rather than comparing themselves to others in the group. Even though some element of competition is almost inevitable, it can be discouraging for the weaker members of a good group, who are steadily achieving the course objectives, to compare themselves with the best.

Positive feedback

Learners will very soon get used to reflecting critically on their progress, and it can add a new dimension to the learning, but self evaluation does not replace tutor evaluation and it is still essential for the tutor to comment, feed back and praise regularly.

Any serious attempt to involve learners should include the opportunity for them to express what they feel about the class and the methods, materials and activities used.

Feedback

Course evaluation is now standard practice in most colleges, and is generally carried out by means of questionnaires which are circulated at one or two key points during the course. Students comment on their experiences and their responses are analysed and fed back to tutors and organisers. Although the feedback from the questionnaires provides useful information for planning courses for the following year, if we really want to involve current students and ensure that they continue to come to classes, we need to organise something additional which is more personal, more interactive and less official. We need to convince them that asking for their opinion is not merely a formality.

Any open evaluation of the course needs delicate handling. Discussion must be kept focused, positive and constructive if it is to be successful. Left to drift, it can all too easily degenerate into a moaning session about issues such as accommodation and car parking which are outside the tutor's influence, and the negative impression created will certainly not motivate.

Keep it positive

A good alternative to a general discussion is the use of a visual such as the grid illustrated on the following page. It is based on an idea called Repgrid (Rowsell, 1992), and has several advantages.

Focus for discussion

- It is an interesting class activity which can be carried out entirely in the target language with more advanced learners, and in a mixture of English and the target language with others. Even with learners at the early stages, the constructs can be in the target language, and it then becomes a vocabulary booster.
- It provides a focus for the discussion and gives the tutor the opportunity to bring in some of the reasoning behind the teaching methods (it will probably be necessary to do this in English).
- Using numbers allows learners to express degrees of feeling without necessarily having to be very articulate.
- The completed grids supply tutors with a wealth of information and fascinating insight into the learners' perceptions of the course. It allows them to react sensitively to the group and to nip any potential problems in the bud. It is also a great boost for the tutor if the feedback is positive and only reveals minor negative factors.

5	Listening to explanations	Working in pairs	Working in groups	Working alone	Teacher asking questions to everyone	Teacher asking me questions	Listening to a cassette	Watching a video	Talking about the country	**1**
I like										I don't like
Useful										Not useful
Interesting										Boring
Easy										Difficult
Helpful										Not helpful
I feel comfortable										I feel uncomfortable

1. You need a blank grid for each learner and a copy on acetate for yourself.
2. Prompt learners to name as many different elements of a typical lesson as they can, and agree which should go across the top of the grid.
3. Down the left hand side, list as many different constructs as you can think of to describe how the students might feel about those elements.
4. On the right hand side, write the opposites of these.
5. Learners then go on to discuss how they feel about the lesson elements listed, and fill the grid on a scale of 5–1, where 5 means they agree with the construct on the left, and 1 means they agree with the construct on the right. Any number in between therefore signifies a less certain attitude one way or another.

Timing

The timing of any such discussion is important. The tutor is the best person to gauge the optimum time, but the following are useful guidelines.

- A summative evaluation carried out at the end of the course cannot possibly have any effect on retention rates since the very people who were dissatisfied with their course, i.e. those who dropped out, are not there to comment. It is salutary to reflect that they might have stayed if they had had the opportunity to express their views.
- If it is carried out too early in the year, learners will not have had enough experience on which to base their opinions and could feel threatened by being asked for an opinion they feel unqualified to give.
- It needs to be done early enough for the tutor to be able to react if the survey reveals dissatisfaction.

There is no reason to restrict this to once during the course; it can also be used to diagnose problems at any time in the course, especially if numbers are starting to drop.

Letters

Another means of inviting feedback is by letter. Learners who may not contribute much during a discussion may prefer this alternative. This is best done at a natural break during the course, such as the end of a topic, half-term or the end of the first term.

A letter has the advantage that it can also be sent to anyone who has been absent, and can be the spur they need to come back to the course. The main disadvantage is that it does not allow the tutor to clarify and explain any specific points.

Writing a letter is essentially a personal matter, and the content, the style and the tone depend entirely on the relationship between tutor and learners. What would be right for one person would not be acceptable to another. We do, however, provide below an example of a letter which has been used satisfactorily and which has supplied the tutor with invaluable information from her learners. Not only that, but everyone expressed their satisfaction on being involved in this way.

Over to you

Task 1	Consider the learners in your classes. How do you ensure that they feel involved in their course? How much responsibility do they take for their learning?
Task 2	List any elements of your course which are a direct consequence of learner demand.
Task 3	Other than the examples offered on p55, how many ways of evaluating progress can you think of?
Task 4	Design your own version of Repgrid.
Task 5	Draft a letter (see opposite) to invite your learners to give you their views on your course — either on the course as a whole or on specific aspects of it.

Dear

You are already one third of the way through your course. Perhaps you could take a few moments over the Christmas break to assess the course so far.

Rather than giving you a long questionnaire, I thought I'd just ask each of you to write down a few ideas you might have to improve the course and your progress in German over the coming months.

- What aspects of the way I teach do you like and what are you not so keen on?

  _____

  _____

  _____

- What about the materials, worksheets, books, etc used?

  _____

  _____

  _____

- How do you feel the group work, partner work goes? Are you happy with the people you work with?

  _____

  _____

  _____

- Do you know how to talk about your own, and ask about others' holiday activities, hobbies and daily lives? What have you learnt to do that you couldn't do before? What else would you like to do?

  _____

  _____

  _____

Please write down any thoughts you have. They will be treated in the strictest confidence. If you'd rather ring me at home (not Christmas day!), my telephone number is 00 000 000.

Merry Christmas

With thanks to M Boydell

Troubleshooting

Chapter 7

This chapter focuses on problems which relate directly to retention rates, and suggests strategies to overcome or cope with those problems.

We start by considering what options are open to tutors when their learners have missed some classes and might or might not be intending to return. We then go on to feature some of the most common reasons people give for dropping out of language classes, and suggest strategies tutors can employ to deal with them.

Missed classes

There will always be occasions when learners have to miss classes, and once the routine of regular attendance is interrupted, it can be hard to regain the momentum. Making up the ground they lose by missing a class can be enormously difficult for some people and, having found on their return that they cannot cope with the next lesson, they can feel inadequate and uncomfortable. All too often, especially in the case of the less confident learner, the easiest solution can be to stop coming altogether.

The problem affects all levels, but is particularly acute for beginners since the learning curve is at its steepest, and one missed lesson early on in the course represents a large percentage of the total class hours.

Learners who have missed two or three consecutive classes

When a learner has missed two or three consecutive classes, tutors in many colleges are now required to follow them up, to find out why they are not attending and to encourage them to return. Many tutors find this difficult and some indeed feel that if learners cannot be bothered to turn up to a class, then that is their own problem. They worry about intruding, about interfering and about the reception they might receive.

In the vast majority of cases, this worry is misplaced. It also misses the point — it is the learner who is important here and takes precedence over tutor sensibilities.

One should never assume that people are staying away because they no longer want to learn the language or because they don't like the classes. They may have missed a week or two because of illness and are shy of coming back because they feel that they will have missed too much. They may feel that they are not very good; they may even feel that the tutor or the rest of the class would prefer them to stay away rather than hold everyone back. They are probably very disappointed to have 'failed' and will simply not know whether to come back or not.

Making contact is best done sooner rather than later. The longer the period of absence, the more difficult it becomes to re-integrate a learner into the class. The aim is to give these learners another chance, to take the initiative in making it easier for them to come back after an absence. The way it is done is dependent on the relationship between tutor and learner. There can be no set of rules and the following are no more than suggestions.

By telephone

Ring them up, explain that you are concerned about their absence, and tell them what ground the class have been covering in the meantime.

Most will be delighted at your concern, will offer a simple explanation and express their intention to return. Some will have reservations as already mentioned, and you will have to reassure them that all is not lost and specify some work for them to do at home before they come back.

If anyone seems hesitant and appears to be worried or embarrassed about some aspect of the course, this can be a good opportunity to find out why. Some people find it easier to explain over the telephone as it seems less personal.

If anyone has obviously no intention of coming back and shows no inclination to discuss the matter, ask them if they would mind helping you by completing a short questionnaire about the course. This might at least give you an insight into their reasons for leaving.

A note of caution

When ringing people up, it is best to talk to the person directly and avoid leaving messages, either with other people or on answering machines. It is, after all, a private matter between learner and tutor.

By letter

Send a short note. It can either be a personal letter or a semi-official note on college headed paper like the one illustrated. In either case it has more direct impact if signed by the tutor rather than sent out by a secretary.

G·A·C

Grange Adult Centre

Dear Lynne,

We're sorry that you haven't been able to make it to the class for the last week or two. I hope you'll be able to continue with your course and look forward to seeing you next week.
If there's a problem, please don't hesitate to contact me.

Regards,

Chris

If the contact is to be made at a time when a written evaluation was already planned (p59), the letter or questionnaire can simply be sent out to the absentees. It will be more friendly if a short, hand-written note is sent out with it to indicate that you are hoping to see them back soon.

Involve the group

In a well established group, one of the other students may well offer to contact the person who has been away and take along some notes. This can be the best incentive of all to return, and underlines the importance and the value of creating a group (Chapter 4).

Common problems and strategies

In many instances the suggestions which follow reiterate or reinforce messages found elsewhere in the book, and, where the issue has already been dealt with in some detail, reference is made to the relevant chapter and page.

Missed classes

> I missed a class because of work, and found I couldn't cope when I went back the next week.

> When I went back after being ill, the rest of the class had moved on so much that I couldn't catch up.

STRATEGIES
- Build a revision factor into the classes. Use 'what we did last week' as a warm-up activity.
- Provide back copies of any handouts (or advance copies if you know someone is going to be away).
- Refer them to the relevant section of the coursebook. If they do not have the tapes, encourage them to borrow them from the library.
- If the college has a self-access language centre, suggest a session or two there.
- Present the same language functions or exponents at another time in a different context. Make them aware that they have more than one bite at the cherry.

Dissatisfaction with course content

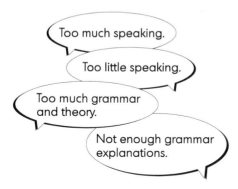

STRATEGIES

- Gain their trust in your competence — explain your methods (p24).
- Make time to talk about the course and allow people the opportunity to express their thoughts. Try Repgrid, p58.
- Ensure an element of negotiation to give everyone a stake in the proceedings. (p54).

Pace of classes too great

STRATEGIES

- Don't underestimate the difficulty of language learning and assume that everyone will cope instantly.
- Build a revision factor into the classes.
- Revisit language functions and exponents in different contexts.
- Ensure students are adequately prepared before you expect them to 'perform'.
- Choral repetition of new language allows students to have a go without feeling threatened.

Misunderstanding of methodology

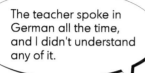

STRATEGIES

- Explain the rationale behind your methods — there are still many misconceptions about target language teaching and many students assume they should understand every single word.
- When addressing learners in the target language, make sure they understand the gist of what is said through exaggerated gestures, expression and paraphrasing.
- Be responsive to learners' feelings and aware of how they are reacting to you.

Classes not lively enough

> We did the same thing every week.

> We just went through the coursebook every lesson, and I could do that at home.

STRATEGIES
- Use a variety of materials, resources and activities. (Chapter 5).
- Don't let any one activity drag on for too long.

If classes are static and lacking in pace and variety, students certainly won't make the effort to turn out, particularly after a hard day at work.

Classes too big

> I don't think the tutor even knew my name when I left.

> The class was enormous, and we spent most of the two hours waiting to speak.

> There was no way I was going to speak in front of twenty other people.

> I never got to know anyone properly.

STRATEGIES
- Right from the start, ensure that tutor and learners have the opportunity to get to know each other (p27).
- Organise plenty of student-centred activities, enabling learners to have more talking time, instead of waiting half an hour for their turn, and then having to 'perform' in front of a sizeable audience.
- Organise small-group and pair work, allowing learners to work with lots of different people.
- Whenever possible, ensure that the room layout is conducive to communication. 25 people crammed into a room in rows is a recipe for disaster.

Class size is a problem which is getting worse rather than better. With minimum numbers higher every year, few centres turn students away, and some classes end up very big indeed. On a positive note, it can often be more fun in a big group, and it is certainly easier to organise interesting activities.

Diverse range of abilities

> It was supposed to be a beginners' class, but most of them knew a lot already.

> There weren't enough students to run a class and so it ended up as a complete mixture of levels.

STRATEGIES
- Ideally everyone should be directed onto the right course at enrolment, but if any have bypassed the system, try to pinpoint them quickly and suggest they transfer to other levels.
- Be firm with anyone who insists on staying in an unsuitable class, and ensure that they do not disrupt the class for the others.
- For mixed-level groups, it is imperative to use a variety of activities so that they can work in pairs or small groups.

*Coping with
the low points*

And finally, the low points. Every course has its peaks and troughs — steep learning curves and seemingly endless plateaux are natural features of language learning. But the adult class also has other highs and lows to contend with, and the low points are surprisingly easy to predict.

Late November, when the initial euphoria is wearing thin and there are many reasons for adults having to miss classes, which leads to the routine of attendance being disrupted:

The start of the January term:

Late February:

Nothing motivates like success, so these are the times to:

- remind them of the progress they have made by getting out the course objectives and ticking off all the outcomes already covered;
- emphasise their achievement by organising an activity integrating several of the topics covered.

Provide some definite reason for them to come back:

- organise a social event, quiz, competition or another of the activities suggested on p39;
- invite them to bring something in the following week — photographs, realia from a holiday, contribution to a group activity.

However rigorous and thorough our approach, it is unlikely that we will ever eliminate problems altogether, given the nature of part-time adult classes and the scant resources. But even if we cannot regulate the size of classes or prevent learners missing lessons, we can at least try to mitigate the effects.

Over to you

Task 1	Focus on some of the problems which students have brought to your attention. On the basis of what you have read, how might you deal with these problems now?
Task 2	Reflect critically and honestly on your own teaching. If you were one of your students, would you turn out on a cold, foggy November evening to attend your language class? If not, why not?

Conclusion

We hope that this book offers some constructive suggestions for improving the chances of students staying the course. Summed up, it is about improving and maintaining the quality of what we offer our learners. No one factor can be pinpointed as the miracle factor, rather it is a combination of factors, a fusion of good practice, expertise and enthusiasm.

Language tutors today are required to have, over and above a good linguistic knowledge and a teaching qualification, the skills of managing a group, producing materials, motivating and inspiring the learners, and the ability to generate that indefinable buzz which is the keystone of a successful language class.

The issue of retention rates should not, however, be the concern of the tutor alone. The managers who insist on an improvement in retention rates have a responsibility to support tutors and to resource adult classes adequately. Classes, now larger than ever before, need appropriate accommodation and resources. Tutors need training and support for that training. We all owe it to our students to lobby for such support.

Success in improving retention rates involves, too, among all the other things, remembering that we are dealing with people, not statistics — and the unpredictability of human nature is perfectly illustrated by the two people questioned in the Mid-Cheshire survey who gave the following reasons for dropping out of their French class.

Appendix

FEFC funding

At the time of writing most adult language classes are funded by the Further Education Funding Council (FEFC) and the following is a brief summary of current funding arrangements for vocational classes.

Funding is calculated in 'units of activity' which have a monetary value. Each student enrolled attracts a certain number of these funding units depending on factors such as the type of course, the course length and the qualification. A college then calculates its budget from the numbers of students enrolled and receives the calculated amount in instalments. Payment is dependent on students' continuing attendance which is monitored. There are three audit dates: 1 November, 1 February and 15 May.

For a typical 60-hour vocational language course starting in September:

- The full amount is only granted for a student who:
  - receives appropriate advice and guidance on entry to the course;
  - has access to all 60 guided learning hours;
  - keeps attending until the end of the course;
  - successfully achieves the recognised qualification for the course.

- No funding at all is received by the college for a student who enrols on a course and then drops out before 1 November.

- Less than 50% of the full amount is granted for a student who drops out of a course between 1 November and 1 February.

- Only 70% of the full amount is granted for a student who drops out of a course between 1 February and 15 May.

Further reading

Ainslie S, *Foreign language courses for adults — the Lancashire survey*. Unpublished report (1991)

Ainslie S, *Mixed-ability teaching: meeting learners' needs* (CILT, 1994)

Ainslie S and A Lamping, *Assessing adult learners* (CILT, 1995)

Arthur L and S Hurd (eds), *The adult language learner: a guide to good teaching practice* (CILT, 1992)

Brown S and P Knight, *Assessing learning in higher education* (Kogan Page, 1994)

Convery A and D Coyle, *Differentiation — taking the initiative* (CILT, 1993)

Hotho Jackson S, 'Motivation and the drop-out factor' in *Language Learning Journal* no 11 (Association for Language Learning, 1995)

Klippel F, *Keep talking* (CUP, 1984)

Langran J and S Purcell, *Language games and activities* (CILT, 1994)

Page B (ed), *Letting go — taking hold: a guide to independent language learning by teachers for teachers* (CILT, 1992)

Sidwell D, *A toolkit for talking: strategies for independent communication* (CILT, 1993)

Ur P, *Discussions that work* (CUP, 1981)

Ur P and A Wright, *Five-minute activities: a resource book of short activities* (CUP, 1992)

Watcyn-Jones P, *Pair work: activities for effective communication* (Penguin, 1981)

CILT publishes a wide range of books relating to language teaching and learning:

- **NETWORD** series: for adult language tutors;
- **Pathfinder** series: focusing on specific issues relating to good classroom practice.

Information on publications and on NETWORD groups is available from CILT, 20 Bedfordbury, London WC2 4LB. Tel: 0171 379 5101 Ext 248.